MW01251082

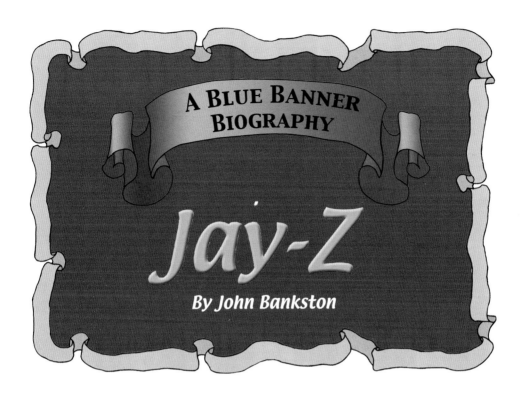

A BLUE BANNER BIOGRAPHY

Jay-Z

By John Bankston

P.O. Box 196
Hockessin, Delaware 19707
Visit us on the web: www.mitchelllane.com
Comments? email us: mitchelllane@mitchelllane.com

Printing   1   2   3   4   5   6   7   8   9

Blue Banner Biographies

Bow Wow	Missy Elliott	Eminem
Sally Field	Ja Rule	**Jay-Z**
Jodie Foster	Melissa Gilbert	Rudy Giuliani
Ron Howard	Michael Jackson	Jennifer Lopez
Nelly	Mary-Kate and Ashley Olsen	Daniel Radcliffe
Selena	Shirley Temple	Ritchie Valens
Rita Williams-Garcia		

Library of Congress Cataloging-in-Publication Data
Cataloging data is available for this book.
ABOUT THE AUTHOR: Born in Boston, Massachussetts, **John Bankston** began publishing articles in newspapers and magazines while still a teenager. Since then, he has written over two hundred articles, and contributed chapters to books such as *Crimes of Passion,* and *Death Row 2000,* which have been sold in bookstores across the world. He has written numerous biographies for young adults, including *Eminem* and *Nelly* (Mitchell Lane). He currently lives in Portland, Oregon.
PHOTO CREDITS: Cover: Todd Plitt/Getty Images; p. 4 Scott Gries/Getty Images; p. 12 John Krondes/Globe Photos; p. 15 AP Photo/Quad-City Times, Sean Gallagher; p. 17 Kevin Winter/Getty Images; p. 21 Scott Gries/ImageDirect/Getty Images; p. 24 Michael Appleton/Corbis Sygma; p. 27 Evan Agostini/Getty Images
ACKNOWLEDGMENTS: The following story has been thoroughly researched, and to the best of our knowledge, represents a true story. While every possible effort has been made to ensure accuracy, the publisher will not assume liability for damages caused by inaccuracies in the data, and makes no warranty on the accuracy of the information contained herein. This story has not been authorized nor endorsed by Shawn Carter (Jay-Z).

CONTENTS

Jay-Z frequently appears on shows such as MTV's *Total Request Live*, but he also makes more serious appearances. In 2003, he traveled around the country visiting high schools to offer scholarships to students and inspire them to succeed.

The Possible Dream

*J*ay-Z stepped from behind the curtain and looked out at the crowd. He wasn't in an arena; he wasn't in a concert. He was at Marshall High School in Chicago, Illinois, and he was about to tell the students how he'd made it.

A surge of teens pushed forward; a few scrambled onto the stage. "Hold up," Jay-Z said calmly. It was March 2003, and the hip-hop star had long ago gotten used to the craziness of some of his fans. But he needed them to be quiet because he needed them to hear what he had to say.

For six months he'd traveled to high schools across the country. Sometimes he was "principal of the day," sometimes he gave free performances. Although he had a new CD out, his appearances weren't about promotion. His company, Roc-A-Fella, was offering scholarship money so that some of the kids he met would be able to afford college. Just as importantly, Jay-Z wanted the kids to embrace their dreams, even if their dreams seemed impossible.

"I'm not going to sit here and lie and tell you that everybody's going to make it if they follow their dreams…," he told the teens at Marshall High. "I came from nothing to owning my own company. It's real and it can happen and it's a long shot. They say when you play with skill, good luck happens."

Jay-Z has been playing with skill most of his life.

The Marcy Projects rest just a stone's throw from the tracks of the J and Z lines of the New York City subway system. Located in the Bedford-Stuyvesant section of Brooklyn, one of the five boroughs of the city, to outsiders it looks like a haven for crime and poverty.

To Jay-Z, the projects were home.

> **With three older siblings looking out for Shawn, it was tough to get into trouble. He managed.**

He was born Shawn Corey Carter on December 4, 1970, to Adnes and Gloria Carter. With an older brother, Eric, and two older sisters, Anne and Mickey, watching out for him, it was tough to get into trouble. He managed.

At four years old, Shawn found an unused ten-speed bike, climbed on, and as he told *Rolling Stone* magazine, "It was really high, but I put my foot through the top bar, so I'm ridin' the bike kinda weird, like sideways." To young Shawn it seemed like the whole block was watching him as he managed to ride down the street. "They couldn't believe this little boy ridin' that big bike like that. That was my first feelin' of bein' famous right there. And I liked it. Felt good."

All his life Shawn tried to re-create that feeling. He soon realized the best way to get his parents' attention was with music. Adnes and Gloria were huge record collectors. The couple shared everything—everything except those records. Every one had a label for either Gloria or Adnes. The best way to get in trouble in the Carter home was to touch one of those records without permission.

On cleaning Saturdays, Gloria opened the windows and blasted funk and soul music over the roar of the vacuum. Outside Shawn would stop whatever game he was playing to listen as the tunes filled his Brooklyn neighborhood. He felt the rhythm in his bones, but his mind was making up different rhymes. Sometimes he'd hear two or three rhymes at

> *Shawn soon realized the best way to get his parents' attention was with music.*

once, all of them competing for attention. He'd jot them down in a favorite green notebook, or whatever else was handy. Like many writers, his imagination worked faster than his pen.

"I used to write all crooked…," he admitted in the same *Rolling Stone* interview. "Then I started running around in the streets, and that's how not writing came about. I was comin' up with these ideas, and I'd write 'em on a paper bag, and I had all these paper bags in my pocket, and I hate a lot of things in my pocket, so I started memorizing and holding it."

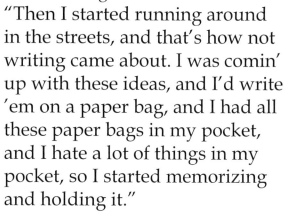

Shawn had a gift for remembering, whether it was the words to a song or lessons in school.

Shawn had a gift for remembering, whether it was the words to a song or lessons in school. Usually when he wasn't practicing rhymes, his nose was in a book—by the time he was in sixth grade he was reading as well as a high school senior.

Books and music gave Shawn an escape when life at home grew difficult. When he was 11, his father left, filling Shawn with rage and confusion. Adnes's abandonment was devastating. In 2003, Shawn was able to put the past behind him and reconcile with his father, just months before his father died of liver problems.

Shawn scored well enough on tests to be admitted to Brooklyn's prestigious George Westinghouse Technical High School. Although his schoolwork was important, it was the friends he made there that helped change his life. Later on, George Westinghouse would become known as Hip-Hop High School for the number of future stars who attended. Among them, Busta Rhymes was a classmate and friend of Shawn's. Still his closest friend was future collaborator Christopher Wallace—a large, deep-voiced teen who would grow up to be known as the Notorious B.I.G.

All three were developing as rappers just as hip-hop music was becoming popular. When he was a kid, Shawn had scribbled down rhymes over the music his mother played. In the 1980s, MCs, or rappers, were doing the same thing professionally. Snippets of popular songs— samples—were played in the background while rap artists rhymed over them. Beginning with groups like the Sugar Hill Gang and the Beastie Boys, hip-hop began getting played on the radio and on MTV in the middle 1980s.

By then Shawn needed all the positive outlets for his creativity that he could find.

In high school, Shawn's classmates included future stars Busta Rhymes and the Notorious B.I.G.

Always Say, "D.I.Y."

Money in the Carter household was tight. Gloria worked long hours as a clerk in a Wall Street investment firm, but her salary barely covered necessities. There were few luxuries in Shawn Carter's life. He learned how to do without, but he never got used to it. Despite his good grades, Shawn worried about the future. At 16 years old, Shawn Carter believed dreams like his cost money.

Outside his Brooklyn home he saw kids his age making fast bucks selling drugs. While he rarely discusses it today, Shawn became a dealer. As he told the short-lived *Blaze Magazine,* "I know from being a hustler that they don't regard rappers as the smartest people... Runnin' around dancin' and rappin', makin everybody money except theyself."

Although he pretended to look down on rappers when he was hustling, it was a front. No matter how hard he tried, he couldn't forget his dreams.

At 18, Shawn finally got the break he was looking for. Shawn, the hip-hop artist who would someday be known across the world as Jay-Z, began working with a rapper named Jaz-O or Big Jaz. An album Jaz-O released contained a popular single called "Hawaiian Sophie," which earned him a lot of airplay in New York. Shawn rapped on Jaz-O's album, *The Originators,* and on another by the group Original Flavor.

Shawn didn't have a contract, he wasn't promised anything. But when Jaz-O asked Shawn if he wanted to join an upcoming tour, the young man was faced with a decision. He wouldn't just have to give up hustling. He'd have to give up George Westinghouse High. He was sure he was on his way to a new career. Unfortunately, Shawn didn't know anything about the business part of the record business.

Shawn began working with rapper Jaz-O. When Jaz-O asked Shawn to tour with him, Shawn was faced with a decision.

He gave up a high school diploma for a high-risk hip-hop career. He toured with Jaz-O and later with Big Daddy Kane. Throughout the experience, Shawn noticed one thing: Jaz-O didn't seem to be making any money. It looked like all the cash from album sales was going straight to the record label. Even worse, without a contract, Shawn realized the opportunities he'd dreamed of weren't coming his way. The experience left him bitter, but it taught him a painful lesson.

If he wanted to succeed he'd have to learn about the business side. When the time was right, he'd make his own album. As the 1990s began, Shawn promised himself he wouldn't be victimized by a record label.

When Jay-Z first started rapping, he promised himself he wouldn't be victimized by a record label. Starting his own company has allowed him to open his own nightclub, the 40/40 club. He is shown here at the grand opening.

That wouldn't be easy. Musicians have a hard time making money. It's not just struggling wannabes who worry about getting paid. Top recording stars share the same concerns. Recording contracts are some of the toughest in the entertainment industry, usually requiring over half a dozen albums from a musician and a commitment of many years. Even a hit single or album doesn't guarantee an artist riches.

In the late 1990s, hip-hop trio TLC went public with their own financial difficulties. Although their albums sold in the millions, the three young women were almost broke. Part of the reason TLC and many other artists have trouble bringing money home is because record labels usually subtract the costs of studio time, videos, and concert tours from the money the artist makes. Labels say this is because they take the risk and lose money on acts that don't become popular. All Shawn knew was that when he finally produced a record, it would be DIY: *Do It Yourself.*

Recording contracts are some of the toughest in entertainment, requiring commitments of many albums and many years.

Instead of going back to hustling, Shawn got a job. "It wasn't specifically one thing," he admitted to *The Washington Post.* "It was more so out of fear. You can't run on the streets forever. What are you going to be doing when you're thirty years old or thirty-five or forty? I had a fear of being nothing that pretty much drove me."

Shawn began working as a fry cook at a fast-food chicken restaurant. It was a huge drop in pay for the former dealer, and it was even harder when he saw young hustlers coming in with money and nice clothes. But he stuck with it. He realized it would be pretty difficult to have a music career in jail. Besides, the job introduced him to Memphis Bleek, a skilled rapper who shared Shawn's hip-hop dreams.

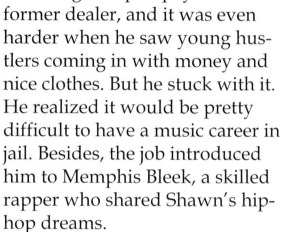

Shawn began working as a fry cook at a fast-food chicken restaurant. He realized he couldn't have a music career in jail.

By 1995, Shawn had saved up enough money to make his dreams real. He cut his own 12-inch single, "In My Lifetime." The record reflected his life growing up in a housing project and dealing drugs as a teen. It was honest and it was raw. Powered by the high-speed rapping skills Shawn had been honing since he was a kid, it featured what he later told *Rolling Stone* were the most important skills a top MC required: "First originality. Narrative—the way you tell a story. They say, 'keepin' it real,' meaning if you could tell a story and it be a true experience, that's a true talent. *Style. Delivery.*"

Shawn's solo debut had all of the above. It also had Shawn promoting it. Whatever sales experience he'd gained hustling, he put to work selling his record. He sold copies from the trunk of his car. He went into nightclubs and asked the DJs to play it; he sold copies to the lines of people outside.

Suddenly Shawn was getting calls from record labels. They said they wanted to help him make a new record. They said they'd let him make the music he wanted to make, with their money behind it. All Shawn could think about was Jaz-O, even as he wondered how far he was going to get selling records out of a car.

Jay-Z promoted his first album by selling copies out of the trunk of his car and asking DJs in nightclubs to play it.

A New Deal

*A*s a teenager, Shawn Carter's friends nicknamed him Jazzy, partly for his slick rhymes and fashion sense. By the time he released his debut album, he was going by Jay-Z, a modification of Jazzy and a shout out to the trains that traveled past his neighborhood. Despite the new name and the confidence he tried to exude, he was still Shawn Carter. He was a guy who'd read a lot of books and kept his eyes open. He saw the dangers of getting involved with a huge music corporation. So when Priority Records offered him a deal, he was reluctant to sign a contract. He'd seen what had happened to his friends.

But Shawn also knew a powerful record label could sell his album all over the world. When Priority Records offered a distribution deal—they'd place the records in stores—and allowed him the freedom to make the record he wanted to make, Shawn accepted.

With his friends Christopher Wallace (The Notorious B.I.G.) and DJ Premier, he made a record every bit as raw as his first lyrically, but one that sounded better because of the money Priority gave him to rent a top recording studio. "It wasn't even like I was making

Although Shawn was reluctant to sign a contract with a record label, he realized that getting his album in stores could get him the publicity he needed.

music," he later told *Rolling Stone*. "The studio was like a psychiatrist's couch for me." Shawn's debut with female rapper Foxy Brown, "Ain't No...," put the name Jay-Z on the Billboard charts for the first time. "Dabbled in crazy weight . . . I'm still spending money from '88," he bragged on the song. Although it was noticed for his high-speed raps and Brown's silky vocals, it came at a time when the use of drug references and offensive language was still the cause of much controversy in popular music. The song was played on radio stations, but only after it was edited.

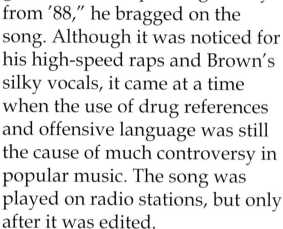

Shawn wasn't happy with the promotion of his debut album, or his share of the profits. He decided to start his own label.

But controversy didn't keep the single from staying at number one on the Billboard Dance Music Maxi-Singles chart for five weeks, an enormous accomplishment for a new artist. The album was released two months later, in June 1996. In just three months it went gold—meaning it sold over 500,000 copies. It would eventually go platinum, selling over one million.

Shawn wasn't satisfied. He knew he could do better. He wasn't happy with the way his debut was promoted, and he wasn't happy with his share of the profits. So Jay-Z decided to put his money where his mouth was.

He decided to start his own label.

Along with partners Biggs Burke and Damon Dash, Shawn's label would do more than just make and sell Jay-Z records. It would also promote new talent, including Shawn's fellow fast-food worker, Memphis Bleek.

Shawn's new label, Roc-A-Fella, quickly signed a deal with Def Jam, the label that helped make LL Cool J a star. Def Jam's job was getting the albums into the stores. Roc-A-Fella would do everything else. If the records sold well, Roc-A-Fella would make most of the money; if they didn't, they'd be the ones who failed.

It was just the way Shawn wanted it.

> *Shawn's label, Roc-A-Fella Records, not only made Jay-Z albums, but also promoted new talent.*

On His Own

Many in the music industry wondered if Shawn "Jay-Z" Carter's new record company could succeed in making and selling Jay-Z music. Their questions were quickly answered.

Beginning in 1997, Roc-A-Fella released a three-album series, *In My Lifetime,* that not only topped record charts but also, because of the generous deal between the label and Def Jam, quickly made Shawn a multimillionaire (by 2003 he was worth over $50 million).

His success let Shawn use music familiar to everyone, not just kids who grew up in neighborhoods like those around the Marcy Projects. When *In My Lifetime*'s Volume 2 debuted at number one on the Billboard Album Charts (it stayed there for five weeks), its success came partly from the song "Hard Knock Life (Ghetto

Anthem)." It used a sample from the musical *Annie* and its song "Hard Knock Life." Shawn had seen the musical as a kid and it stuck with him. "I thought, whoa that's amazing—those kids are too strong to let the ghetto life bring them down!" he told *The Washington Post.* "That's the emotion of the ghetto, that's how people feel right now! Instead of treats we get tricked, instead of kisses we get kicked."

Both Volumes 2 and 3 of *In My Lifetime* reached number one on the Billboard Album Charts. They also earned Shawn a pile of awards.

Among other honors, in 1999 alone he received an award for Lyricist of the Year, Solo at the Source Hip-

Jay-Z has won numerous awards for his work, ranging from best album to artist of the year. Here, he gives a concert for MTV's Unplugged.

Hop Music Awards; Best Rap Video at the MTV Video Music Awards; and a WB Radio Music Award for Song of the Year. Still, for most artists winning a Grammy Award is the highest achievement, and in 1999 Shawn was nominated for three of them.

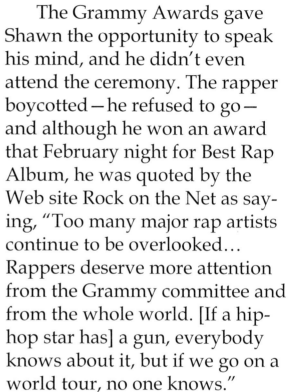

In 1999, Shawn was nominated for three Grammys. He chose to boycott the ceremony, however.

The Grammy Awards gave Shawn the opportunity to speak his mind, and he didn't even attend the ceremony. The rapper boycotted—he refused to go—and although he won an award that February night for Best Rap Album, he was quoted by the Web site Rock on the Net as saying, "Too many major rap artists continue to be overlooked… Rappers deserve more attention from the Grammy committee and from the whole world. [If a hip-hop star has] a gun, everybody knows about it, but if we go on a world tour, no one knows."

The statement seemed to predict the future. Because just ten months later, Jay-Z would be in the news—not for a gun, but for a knife. Although by December 1999 his hard knock life seemed like a distant memory, one violent moment in a nightclub would threaten to take away everything he'd worked so hard to achieve.

Cuts Like a Knife

*W*riters usually write about what they know. Hip-hop stars penning raps aren't any different. Beginning in the late 1980s, many rappers wrote about violence and drugs. Shawn Carter's close friend and collaborator, Christopher Wallace, gained fame as the Notorious B.I.G., or Biggie Smalls. Like Shawn, he'd grown up in Brooklyn and spent his teens as a drug dealer. In interviews, he was often quoted as saying, "You have to die before anyone notices you." His debut album was called *Ready to Die.*

In 1996, Tupac Shakur, who'd gained fame both as a film actor and an MC, was shot to death in Las Vegas. Less than six months later, Wallace was killed in Los Angeles. There were a number of theories about their deaths, including an East Coast/ West Coast rap feud, but the crimes went unsolved. One month after

Jay-Z has worked with Beyoncé Knowles on several songs, including "Crazy in Love" and "'03 Bonnie & Clyde." There has been speculation about Jay-Z and Beyoncé's involvement behind the scenes since the two first collaborated.

Wallace's murder, Wallace's record label released his latest album. It was called *Life After Death*. He'd named it before he was murdered.

The killings pushed many artists away from violent depictions of ghetto life toward songs about money and all it could buy. Shawn's lyrics evolved as well, even as he branched out in his business. Beyond just promoting himself and other artists, his label moved into fashion, beverages, and film.

In December 1999, everything changed. Shawn was with a group of friends and collaborators at New York City's Kit Kat Club, celebrating the new album release from Q-Tip, a fellow rapper. Shawn has just finished celebrating his own release of Volume 3 at another club, and he was in a good mood. Until he entered the Kit Kat.

Among the guests was Lance Rivera, the owner of Untertainment Records. He'd worked as a coproducer on one of Shawn's latest songs, but the two weren't friends.

Shawn believed Rivera was bootlegging his music — selling copies before they hit the stores. Rivera denied this. The tension rose as soon as the two were in the same room, and as one female rapper said in *Newsweek*, "It was clear something was about to go down, because J's attitude changed when he saw Un [Rivera]. They started arguing, and I know these guys all too well. I got … out of the way."

A fight broke out. Versions of the story differ, but before it was over Rivera had been stabbed. He sur-

> *Shawn's label soon went beyond promoting artists, and branched into fashion, beverages, and film.*

vived the injuries and at the hospital pointed the finger at Shawn.

Despite years of rapping about the criminal lifestyle and discussing his drug dealing, Shawn had never been convicted of a crime. Now he was facing multiple assault charges that could put him in jail for 25 years. Shawn claimed he'd never been close to Rivera. As the case dragged on, Shawn did what he always did. He worked.

The next year, his *Dynasty – Roc La Familia 2000* debuted at number one on Billboard's Pop Charts and Shawn scored two more Grammy nominations in 2001. That year Shawn was stunned when his partner Damon Dash's girlfriend, Aaliyah, died in a plane crash. By the end of the year, he just wanted to face the music.

"Where I grew up, I seen a lot of people get wronged," he told *Rolling Stone.* "No matter how much you believe in the truth, that's always in the back of your mind." So in December 2001, Shawn pled guilty to the assault charges and received three years' probation.

Controversy continues to follow Shawn, despite all of his success. While his "principal for a day" events drew thousands of kids, some were offended by it.

Even though Shawn's "principal for a day" events drew thousands of kids, some people were offended by it.

Conservative commentator Bill O'Reilly said on the December 11, 2002, episode of his program, *The O' Reilly Factor,* "He brings a message of the street, and the school really isn't the place for that. The school is to uplift you, educate you, not to teach you how to say the 'F' word fifteen times in a sentence."

Shawn refuses to be slowed by those who are offended. He knows he can bring kids the same message he brings to his extended family: "I tell my nephews that life is about taking chances on yourself, not letting anyone hold you back," he says. "Think big, don't be afraid to fail or to fight harder when things get tough."

Jay-Z has worked with producer Pharrell Williams (left) of the Neptunes on many songs, including "Change Clothes" from The Black Album.

His big dreams have eclipsed his musical career. By 2003, his two clothing lines and the time he spent mentoring young artists at Roc-A-Fella, meant he had less and less time to record. He decided to retire from rapping and planned his last release for Black Friday, the day after Thanksgiving.

Downloads changed the schedule. Just as "The Eminem Show" had its release pushed up the year before, "The Black Album's" launch was bumped up by internet piracy.

"… I hope my fans will support me and Roc-A-Fella Records and buy my final release in an appropriate way," he told *Billboard Magazine*. His fans answered by buying enough copies of his album to secure him the number one position on the charts in his first week. Despite the fact that Jay-Z may never make another album, he will be remembered as a hip-hop legend for years to come.

Shawn's clothing lines and new artists have meant that he has had less and less time to record.

1970 Shawn Carter is born to Adnes and Gloria Carter on December 4 in Brooklyn, New York

1982 father Adnes leaves the family

1988 Shawn tours with Jaz-O

1990 guest raps on albums by Jaz-O and the Originators

1995 produces and sells his own single "In My Lifetime;" gets recording deal with Priority Records; founds Roc-A-Fella Records

1996 releases *Reasonable Doubt* through his own company

1999 boycotts Grammy Awards; is accused of stabbing Lance Rivera

2001 pleads guilty to stabbing; receives probation

2002 is Principal of the Day at high schools across the country

2003 father Adnes dies of liver problems; offers scholarship opportunities to students; collaborates with Beyoncé Knowles on the song "Crazy in Love;" releases "The Black Album" which he claims will be his final record

FOR FURTHER READING

Jay-Z: The Life and Times of Shawn Carter. Rap Life Magazine Staff, ed. MusicnewsTv.com 2001.

Ogg, Alex. *The Men Behind Def Jam: The Radical Rise of Russell Simmons and Rick Rubin*. Omnibus Press, 2002.

On the Web:

MTV.com Bands A-Z: Jay-Z
www.mtv.com/bands/az/jay_z/artist.jhtml

Roc-A-Fella Records
www.rocafella.com

Rock on the Net: Jay-Z
www.rockonthenet.com/artists-j/jayz_main.htm

DISCOGRAPHY

1996	*Reasonable Doubt*
1997	*Vol. 1 – In My Lifetime*
1998	*Vol. 2 – Hard Knock Life*
1999	*Vol. 3 – Life and Times of S. Carter*
2000	*Dynasty – Roc La Familia 2000*
2001	*The Blueprint*
	MTV Unplugged
2002	*Best of Both Worlds*
	The Blueprint 2: The Gift & the Curse
2003	*Blueprint 2.1*
	The Black Album

SELECTED AWARDS

1998   *Rolling Stone* magazine—Best Hip-Hop Artist of the Year
        Grammy Award—Best Rap Album
1999   Nominated for Grammy Award—Best Rap Solo
            Performance
        Nominated for Grammy Award—Best Rap Performance by
            a Duo or Group
        Source Hip-Hop Music Award—Lyricist of the Year
        MTV Video Music Award—Best Rap Video
        Radio Music Award—Song of the Year
        Billboard Music Award—Rap Artist of the Year
2000   Nominated for American Music Award—Favorite Rap/Hip-
            Hop Artist
        Nominated for MTV Video Music Award—Best Rap Video
        Radio Music Award—Artist of the Year: Hip-Hop
2001   Nominated for Grammy Award—Best Rap Performance by
            a Duo or Group
        Nominated for Grammy Award—Best Rap Album
        Nominated for Soul Train Music Award—Best R & B, Soul
            or Rap Album
        Soul Train Music Award—Sammy Davis Jr. Entertainer of
            the Year
        Nominated for Blockbuster Entertainment Award—Favorite
            Artist, Rap
        BET Award—Best Male Hip-Hop Artist
        Nominated for MTV Video Music Award—Best Rap Video
        Source Award—Artist of the Year, Solo
2002   Nominated for three Grammy Awards—Best Rap Solo
            Performance, Best Rap Performance by a Duo or
            Group, and Best Rap Album
        Soul Train Music Award—Album of the Year

INDEX